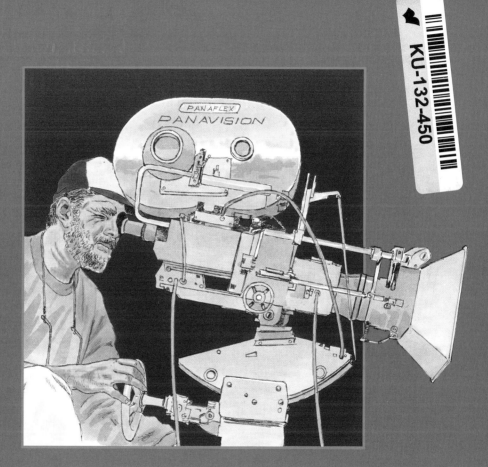

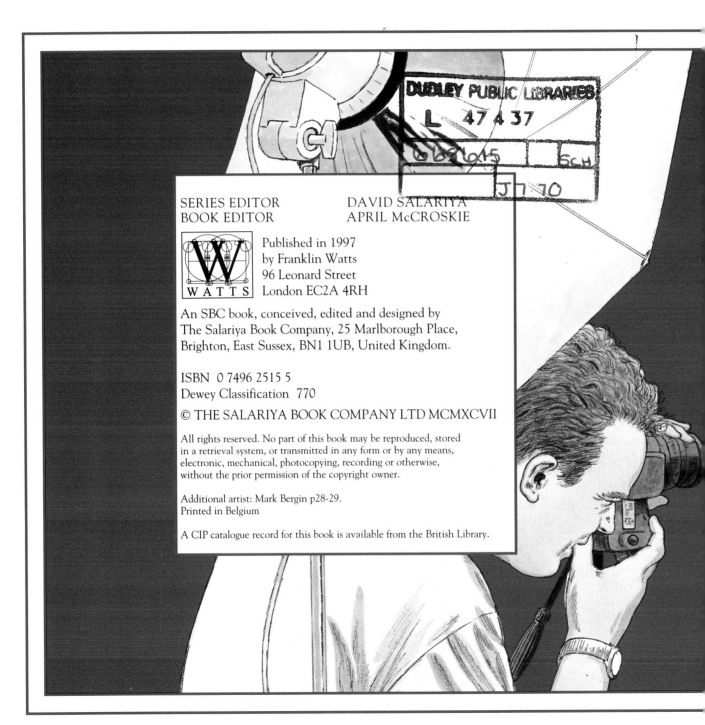

SERIES EDITOR   DAVID SALARIYA
BOOK EDITOR   APRIL McCROSKIE

Published in 1997
by Franklin Watts
96 Leonard Street
London EC2A 4RH

An SBC book, conceived, edited and designed by
The Salariya Book Company, 25 Marlborough Place,
Brighton, East Sussex, BN1 1UB, United Kingdom.

ISBN 0 7496 2515 5
Dewey Classification 770

© THE SALARIYA BOOK COMPANY LTD MCMXCVII

Additional artist: Mark Bergin p28-29.
Printed in Belgium

A CIP catalogue record for this book is available from the British Library.

photography & film

Written by
IAN GRAHAM

Illustrated by
NICHOLAS HEWETSON

Series Created & Designed by
DAVID SALARIYA

W
FRANKLIN WATTS
LONDON • NEW YORK • SYDNEY

CONTENTS

Introduction 7

The Earliest Photography 8

The First Uses of Photography 10

Victorian Photography 12

Inside a Camera 14

Light and Lenses 16

How Film Works 18

Instant Pictures 20

Different Types of Camera 22

In the Studio 24

Spy Photography and X-rays 26

Moving Pictures 28

Filming a Scene 30

Putting it all Together 32

Special Effects 34

Playing With Time 36

Useful Words 38

Index 39

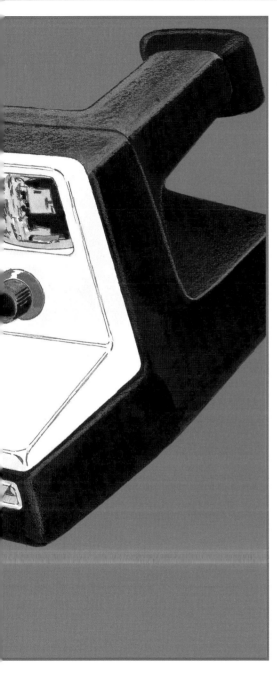

Photography is all around

us. Photographs make newspapers and magazines more colourful and interesting. They record important events in our lives such as holidays and birthdays. They show us people, places and objects that we cannot see with our own eyes. Films reveal pictures from underneath the oceans, events in distant places, or even out in space.

When photography began, cameras were big, heavy, wooden boxes. Modern cameras are small, light and easy to use. Anyone can be a photographer now.

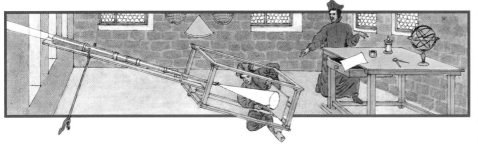

Many who used camera obscuras were church people. They were among the few educated people of early times.

The first photograph was made by Joseph Nicéphore Niepce in 1826. His 'film' was a metal plate inside a camera obscura.

The oldest surviving photograph is a view from Niepce's window taken in 1827. The plate inside his camera was exposed for eight hours.

Camera obscura

Niepce takes his first photograph.

In 1829 Niepce teamed up with Louis Jacques Daguerre. But Niepce died four years later. In 1839 Daguerre invented a new way of making photographs. The new method and the photographs were named Daguerreotype.

Around one thousand years ago,

Arab scientists studied the sun using a camera obscura. Camera obscura means 'dark box'. Sunlight entered a hole in the box and fell upon a screen. But there was no way of keeping the pictures it showed. By the 16th century, the hole had been replaced by a lens. In the 19th century, pictures could be kept by placing a sheet of light-sensitive material inside the box.

The modern camera had been invented.

If you wanted to have your photograph taken with this Daguerreotype camera, you would have to keep still for at least 20 minutes.

A Daguerreotype photograph was made on a silver-coated copper plate. The plate was made sensitive to light by treating it with iodine vapour.

Photographs

allowed people to see images of distant places that they might never visit. They could see what people from other countries looked like and how they dressed. Photographs also showed them how rich and poor people lived.

Early photographers took their cameras to war. They had to take their darkroom with them too, with all the chemicals needed to process the photographic plates. For the first time, photographs showed people what war was like.

Photographs of the Crimean War in the 1850s, were processed inside a horse-drawn darkroom.

Photographs of people and places taken by early photographers are now important historical records.

Photographs let people see other parts of the world long before holidays abroad were common.

When small easy-to-use cameras became available, people could take their own photographs.

Victorian children were the first to collect photographs of their family and friends in an album.

Daguerre

announced that he had invented photography and within a couple of years people were flocking to have their photograph taken. Photographic studios opened in many towns. Having a photograph taken in a studio was such a special occasion that people usually wore their best suit or dress. People often look stiff in Victorian photographs. This is because they had to stay still for so long that it was difficult to look relaxed. It was also hard to smile for such a long time, so they often look quite glum.

The brown colour of a sepia print is a good clue that a photograph could be very old.

Victorian photographs are often tinted a brown colour called sepia. It was made from the liquid squirted out by a sea creature called a cuttlefish.

Glass plates were used in Victorian cameras. They needed more light to form an image than film does today. Exposures of up to 40 seconds were necessary.

The subject had to keep still during the exposure otherwise the photograph would be blurred. Neck supports helped them to keep still.

The photographer checks the image before taking a photograph. A black cloth pulled over his head makes it easier for him to see.

Black cloth

The background in a studio photograph was often painted on canvas. A studio might have a selection of backgrounds.

The Box Brownie was the first camera designed for ordinary people. Millions of them were bought when they went on sale in 1900.

Tripod

Photographer

Plate cameras were named after the glass plates they used instead of film. A plate was needed for each photograph.

The Box Brownie was easy to use. Instead of glass plates, it used roll film which was sent away for processing.

A **camera** is a light-proof box. A hole in the front (the aperture) lets light pass through and fall on the film inside. When the camera is not being used, a shutter is closed tightly over this hole, keeping the film in total darkness. When you press a button, the shutter opens. Light enters the lens at the front and is directed through the hole, forming a clear image on the film. The shutter then closes again and the film is wound on, ready for the next photograph.

Taking a photograph is very simple. The viewfinder shows you the picture you are about to take. When you have lined up the camera, press the shutter release button. After a fraction of a second, the shutter will snap shut again.

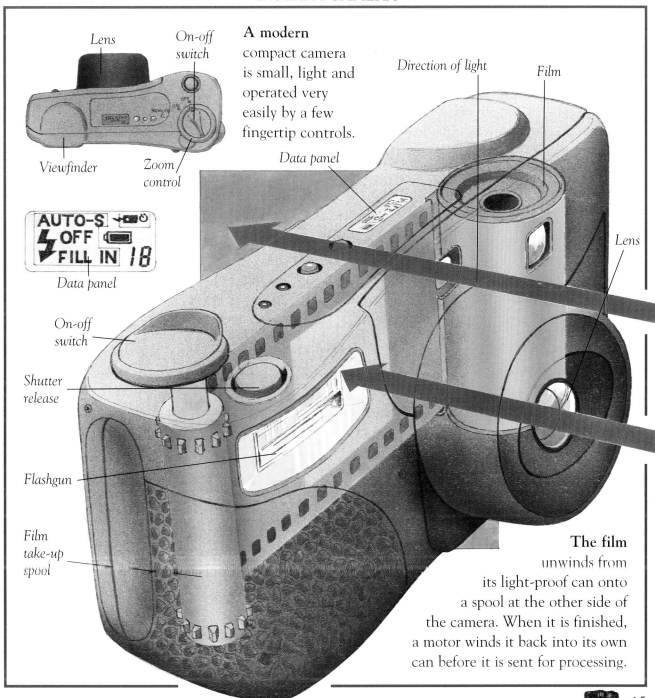

Lens

On-off switch

Viewfinder

Zoom control

A modern compact camera is small, light and operated very easily by a few fingertip controls.

Data panel

Direction of light

Film

Lens

AUTO-S
OFF
FILL IN 18

Data panel

On-off switch

Shutter release

Flashgun

Film take-up spool

The film unwinds from its light-proof can onto a spool at the other side of the camera. When it is finished, a motor winds it back into its own can before it is sent for processing.

15

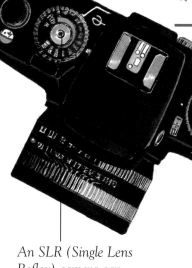

Aperture size is described by a measurement called an f-number. A big number means a small aperture. So, f/16 is smaller than f/4.

f/4

f/16

Lenses bend light rays. A telephoto lens bends light more and produces a bigger image than a wide-angle lens.

The correct

amount of light must strike the film to make a perfect photograph. There are two ways of controlling the amount of light entering a camera. Changing the shutter speed varies the length of time that the shutter is open. Changing the aperture alters the size of the hole that lets light into the front of the camera. Most cameras can set shutter speed and aperture automatically.

An SLR (Single Lens Reflex) camera can be fitted with different lenses. The shutter speed is adjusted by a dial on top of the camera.

Wide-angle lens

Automatic setting

Telephoto lens

A flashgun is used if it is dark. When the camera's shutter release button is pressed, a switch closes and lights up the flashgun. An automatic flashgun measures the amount of light reflected back to it and it adjusts the power and length of the flash.

Some cameras already have a flashgun fitted inside them. If a camera does not have a built-in flashgun, one can be added. It is clipped into a socket, called an accessory shoe, on top of the camera.

The flash head can be tilted so that it points in different directions.

Moveable flash head

Flash tube

Capacitor

Hot shoe

Accessory shoe

When an automatic flashgun fires, a sensor picks up the light reflected back to it. It turns the light into an electrical signal which controls the flash.

Light sensor

A flashgun is connected to a camera by a 'sync lead' or by electrical contacts in the accessory shoe. The shoe is then known as a hot shoe.

Sync lead

Batteries

If a camera has no hot shoe for connecting a flashgun, a detachable hot shoe can be fitted.

Power from batteries is boosted by an instrument called a capacitor. The power is then turned into light by the flash tube.

There are three popular types of film.

When film is struck by light its coating, called the emulsion, changes. Colour film has three light-sensitive layers. One is sensitive to red light, the second to green light and the third to blue light.

When film is treated with chemicals, three coloured images form on top of each other. To make a photograph, or print, light is shone through the film onto light-sensitive paper. The paper is then treated with the same chemicals as the film to produce the finished print.

Black and white film and colour negative film are used to make photographs. Reversal film is used to make slides, for projection onto a screen.

Colour negative film

When colour film is developed, the colours are reversed. This is called a 'negative'. When a photograph is made from this negative the colours are reversed again and look correct.

Photographic prints are made using an enlarger. It has a compartment for the film and a light to project the film onto a baseboard. The height control makes the image appear larger or smaller and a focusing knob controls how clear it is.

Film compartment

Focusing knob

Height control

Light inside the enlarger projects the negative onto photographic paper, which is on the baseboard.

Developing chemicals

When the picture is fully developed, a stop bath stops the developer working.

The paper is taken from the enlarger and placed in a tray containing the developing chemicals. As the developer washes over it, the picture begins to appear.

The photograph is soaked in fixer to make it permanent.

A photographer makes a print using an enlarger in a dimly lit darkroom.

Baseboard

The photograph is washed in fresh water to get rid of all the chemicals.

Photographs from an instant picture camera begin to develop as they leave the camera.

A photo booth produces a strip of head-and-shoulders photographs within a few minutes of taking the pictures.

As the photograph leaves the camera, it is coated with chemicals that develop the picture.

Film usually has to be sent to a processing laboratory to be developed and turned into a set of photographs. But an instant picture camera uses a special type of film that develops and turns into photographs, by itself. Each photograph slides out of a slot as soon as the picture is taken. It is fully developed in about a minute.

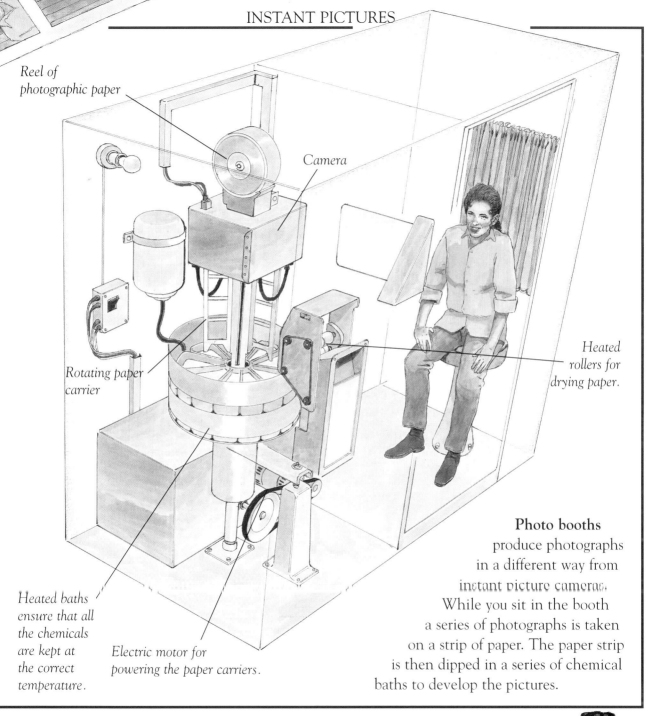

Reel of
photographic paper

Camera

Rotating paper
carrier

Heated
rollers for
drying paper.

Heated baths
ensure that all
the chemicals
are kept at
the correct
temperature.

Electric motor for
powering the paper carriers.

Photo booths
produce photographs
in a different way from
instant picture cameras.
While you sit in the booth
a series of photographs is taken
on a strip of paper. The paper strip
is then dipped in a series of chemical
baths to develop the pictures.

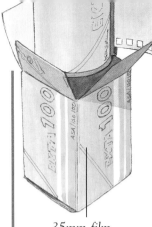

35mm film

*Medium
format
camera*

There are several different types of camera. The most popular are the compact camera and the single lens reflex (SLR) camera. A compact camera is small enough to fit into a bag or pocket. It is very easy to use – just aim using the viewfinder and press the button. An SLR gives the photographer more control over shutter speed, aperture and focus. An SLR can also be fitted with a variety of lenses.

*A
disposable
camera is used only
once. The whole
camera is sent away,
with the film inside,
for processing.*

Camera with

Most cameras use 35mm film with a negative that is 36mm by 24mm. A medium format camera has a negative that is 60mm by 60mm.

*Light follows
a complicated
path as it
travels
through a
single lens
reflex camera.*

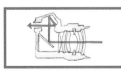

*Light bounces off a
mirror up to the top
of the camera and
through the eyepiece.*

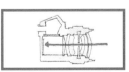

*When the shutter
release is pressed, the
mirror flips up and
the diaphragm closes.*

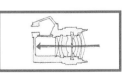

*Next, the shutter
opens, allowing light
to pass through and
fall on the film.*

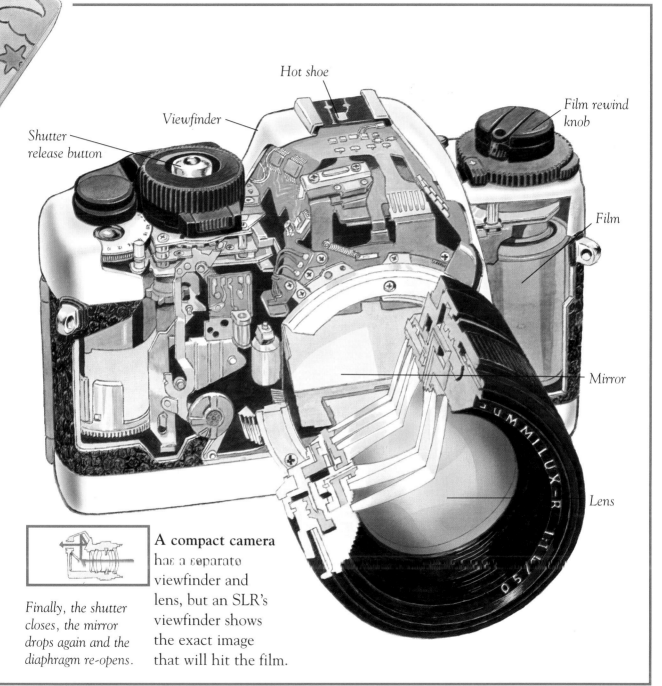

Hot shoe

Viewfinder

Film rewind knob

Shutter release button

Film

Mirror

Lens

A compact camera has a separate viewfinder and lens, but an SLR's viewfinder shows the exact image that will hit the film.

Finally, the shutter closes, the mirror drops again and the diaphragm re-opens.

The word photograph comes from two Greek words, *phos* and *graphos*, meaning 'writing with light'. Good lighting is very important, so photographers often work in a studio where everything is under their control. By combining a number of lights in different ways, the photographer can create the impression of different moods or atmospheres. An attractive background or special effects such as wind, a shower of rain or an eerie carpet of fog, can help to produce almost any image the photographer wants. Professional photographers often use an instant picture camera to check that everything looks just right before they take the photograph on normal film.

Like Victorian studios, modern studios have a selection of backgrounds to choose from.

Flash unit

Model

Reflector

Flash lighting can be too strong, so studio flash units are often pointed at large reflectors to spread and soften the light.

A studio flash unit can be set off by a cable connected to the camera or by the light of another flash unit. The main flash unit connected to the camera is the 'master' unit. Flash units set off by light are 'slave' units. They are fitted with light sensors. When the master unit flashes, the light detected by sensors sets off the slave units.

If the camera moves, the photograph will be blurred. A studio camera is fixed to a tripod to hold it steady.

Tripod

As a model poses, the photographer must choose the right moment to open the shutter and take the best picture.

25

Doctors use X-ray photographs to look inside patients for problems that cannot be seen from outside their bodies.

The black rods that appear in an X-ray photograph prove that this statue is a fake made from parts of other statues.

Photography is sometimes used to see things that cannot normally be seen. Cameras carried by spy planes and satellites take secret photographs from great heights. X-rays produce photographs from inside people and objects. As X-rays pass through a hospital patient, they are blocked by bone, but they can pass through skin and muscle more easily. On the other side of the patient the X-rays strike a sheet of photographic film. When the film is developed, it is dark wherever the X-rays have struck it. The result is a shadow picture of the patient's bones.

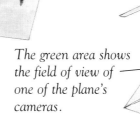

The green area shows the field of view of one of the plane's cameras.

Spy plane

Spy planes often take photographs on heat-sensitive infra-red film. Hot objects appear lighter than cooler objects.

1.

2.

3.

4.

Spy planes fly at heights of more than 20,000 metres to avoid being spotted while they take photographs.

Weather satellites fly around the earth taking photographs from space. They send the photographs back to earth using radio signals. The photographs help experts predict the weather.

Satellite photographs are processed by computer. The photograph of Scotland (1) shows where to find uranium. The photograph showing minerals (2) and the photograph showing rock formations (3) can be combined to show the best places to drill (4).

An enlargement from part of a photograph taken by the Meteosat 3 satellite. It shows cloud patterns over Europe and North Africa.

In the 1830s, people had toys that made a series of printed pictures on a spinning disc, or drum, look like one moving picture. Each picture was slightly different from the one before. When seen quickly, one after another, they merged to form a single moving image. When photography was invented, the printed pictures were replaced by photographs on a long strip of film. This was the beginning of the cinema industry.

In the 1600s, painted glass slides were projected onto a screen. These were called magic lantern shows.

By the 1800s, the images were made to grow and shrink by moving the lantern forwards and back.

In 1891, Thomas Edison invented the kinetoscope – a machine showing a film lasting 15 seconds. People watched it through the machine's peephole.

CINEMATOGRAPHE LUMIÈRE

This poster was put up in Paris in 1895 by two French brothers, Auguste and Louis Lumière. The poster was to attract people to the world's first public showing of a film.

Most early films were made outside in natural daylight because artificial lighting was so expensive to use. Even indoor scenes were filmed outdoors, in specially-built rooms. They had no ceilings and could let in lots of light.

Charlie Chaplin was one of the first, most famous and best-loved stars of silent films. He appeared in many of his films dressed as a tramp wearing shabby clothes and carrying a cane.

Chaplin

In 1927, cinema audiences watched the film The Jazz Singer. *They were the first people to hear an actor, Al Jolson, talking from the cinema screen.*

In 1900 the British film-maker, George Smith, converted his greenhouse into a film studio so that he could make films in daylight – even when it was raining.

Hand-cranked camera

Converted greenhouse

The first movie cameras were worked by hand. The operator turned a handle, or crank, to wind the film through the camera.

In the 1920s and 1930s, people flocked to the large, modern and luxurious cinemas that were built in Europe and the USA.

29

Nowadays, many 'outdoor' scenes that appear in films are filmed indoors. Studios have lighting that mimics daylight.

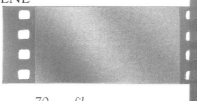

70mm film

35mm film

A film crew combines the skills of sound, camera and lighting equipment operators, and technicians working together as a team.

The width of film and the shape of the image on it is called the film format. In the 1950s, 70mm was popular. Today, 35mm is standard. The largest format is IMAX – ten times the size of 35mm film.

Each new scene in a film begins with the loud crack of a clapperboard being snapped closed in front of a camera.

The words of actors and actresses are picked up by a microphone on a long pole called a boom.

PROD. RUNAWAY
DIR/CAM BILL SHOT 2ND UNIT
SLATE 31 90 TAKE 2

IMAX film

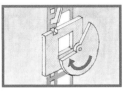

Film moves through a movie camera with a start-stop motion. While it is still, the shutter is open.

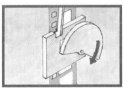

When the spinning shutter closes, a 'claw' pulls the film through ready for the next picture.

The shutter opens again and the whole process then repeats itself.

When a scene is ready to be filmed, a tape machine – to record the sound – and a camera are started.

A clapperboard is snapped closed in front of the camera and the director shouts 'Action!' When the film is edited later, the sound of the clapperboard on the tape can be matched to its picture on the film. This makes sure that the sound and pictures in the finished film match each other.

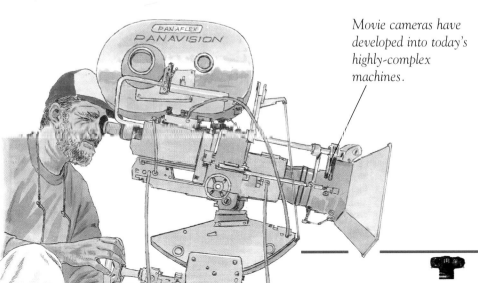

Movie cameras have developed into today's highly-complex machines.

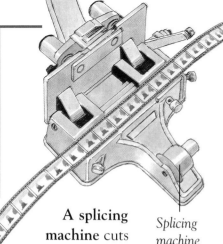

The many scenes

that make up a movie might not be filmed in the same order in which they will appear in the cinema. They are put together in the right order by a film editor. A film editor takes each piece of film and joins it to the others. The lengths of film are joined together using a splicing machine. Some scenes may be shortened by cutting out a piece of the film. Some scenes may not be used at all. Then the sound of the actors' voices, special sound effects and music are added later to form the completed film.

A splicing machine cuts the ends of the film so that they can be stuck together neatly with sticky tape.

Splicing machine

Movies are stored as large reels of film inside metal cans.

The title of the film is written on tape and stuck on each can.

After all the scenes have been filmed and all the sounds and music recorded, a film is like a huge jigsaw puzzle. The director, film editor and sound mixer must decide how many pieces of film they will use and how they will put them together.

Film sounds are played on a huge tape recorder and transferred onto one tape.

Viewing screen

Editing table

Film editor

The soundtrack is created at a mixing desk. Sound levels are adjusted and special effects, like echoes, are added.

The edited film and soundtrack is checked in small sections called cuts. This is done at an editing table with its own small viewing screen.

Sound mixer

Mixing desk

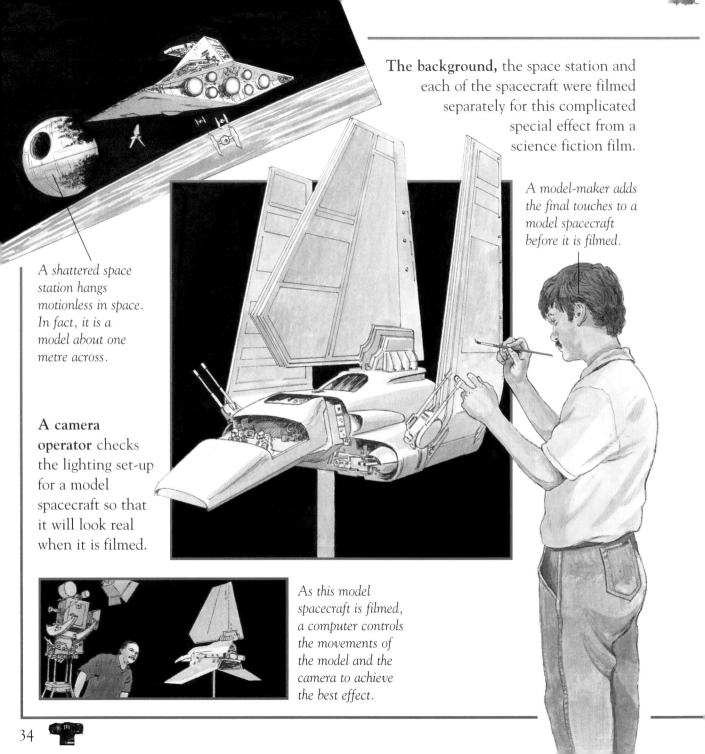

The background, the space station and each of the spacecraft were filmed separately for this complicated special effect from a science fiction film.

A model-maker adds the final touches to a model spacecraft before it is filmed.

A shattered space station hangs motionless in space. In fact, it is a model about one metre across.

A camera operator checks the lighting set-up for a model spacecraft so that it will look real when it is filmed.

As this model spacecraft is filmed, a computer controls the movements of the model and the camera to achieve the best effect.

Special effects have been used by film makers to trick audiences since the first films were made. Special effects can create places that never existed and show events that never happened. Yet they look real when they appear on the cinema screen. Tiny models can be made to look like enormous buildings or planets flying through space. Film of live actors can be combined with a background painted by an artist or created by a computer. Even dinosaurs and space monsters can be brought to life on the cinema screen.

Computers can now produce such high-quality images that they are being used to create special effects in films. Here, a dinosaur is being created on a computer for a film.

Each character begins as an outline drawn on a plastic sheet called a cel.

Clay puppets are often used in animated films. The clay can be re-shaped after each photograph is taken. The expression on a puppet's face can be changed to match an actor's voice.

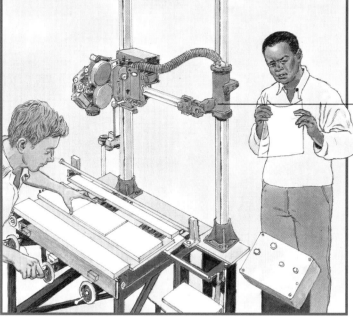

The simple outline is filled in with colour painted on the back of the see-through cel.

Film cels are placed beneath a film camera called a rostrum camera. This takes a still photograph of each cel.

The camera and the cels can be moved by a computer to mimic camera movements used in live action films.

Animated films can bring

paintings or puppets to life. Events that are normally too fast to be seen can be slowed down or stopped. Events that happen too slowly can be speeded up. The secret is the time interval between the photographs.

The mouse cels are photographed on top of another cel with the background.

The movements of the cartoon character are carefully planned to match the soundtrack that has been recorded.

The photofinish camera is often used to reveal who has won a particularly close-run race.

The photograph taken by a photofinish camera can separate athletes who finish a race less than one second apart.

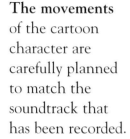

Speeding up the camera makes things appear in slow motion when the film is shown. Running the camera slowly speeds things up when the film is shown.

The way a bird's wings move can be seen clearly if the bird is filmed with a high speed camera. The film shows the wings beating in slow motion.

37

USEFUL WORDS

Aerial photography Taking photographs of the ground with a camera carried in an aeroplane.

Animation Making puppets or painted characters appear to move as if they were real.

Aperture Hole at the front of a camera which controls the amount of light reaching the film.

Cel Sheet of clear plastic on which a cartoon character is painted.

Emulsion Light-sensitive coating on photographic film and paper.

Exposure Uncovering photographic film or paper so that light can reach it.

Flashgun Device inside a camera, or clipped to it, that produces a bright flash of light when it is too dark to take photographs.

Focusing Adjusting a lens so that it forms a clear, sharp picture on the film.

Negative Picture formed on photographic film in which bright parts appear dark and dark parts appear bright.

Shutter Part of a camera that opens to let light reach the film.

Shutter release Button that is pressed to open the shutter and take a photograph.

Soundtrack Sound recording heard when a film is shown.

Splicing Joining one piece of film to another.

Viewfinder Part of a camera that a photographer looks through to aim the camera.